W9-DDA-102

FEB 11 1996

MAR 0 4 1996
DEC 0 2 1996

APR 2 9 1999

AUG 2 6 2002

B&T   9/95

J978.02G

RANCH DRESSING

RANCH DRESSING

The Story of Western Wear

M. Jean Greenlaw

Lodestar Books

Dutton   New York

to my Texas students and friends, who gave me support
and wouldn't let me give up

Library of Congress Cataloging-in-Publication Data
Greenlaw, M. Jean.
   Ranch dressing: the story of western wear/by M. Jean Greenlaw.—1st ed.
     p. cm.
   Includes bibliographical references and index.
   Summary: Discusses the development of the fashion known as western
wear, including such apparel as hats, shirts, jeans, boots, and accessories.
   ISBN 0-525-67432-2
   1. Costume—West (U.S.)—History—Juvenile literature.
   [1. Costume—West (U.S.)—History.] I. Title.
   GT617.W47G74 1993
   391'.00978—dc20   93-15110 CIP AC

Published in the United States by Lodestar Books,
an affiliate of Dutton Children's Books,
a division of Penguin Books USA Inc.,
375 Hudson Street, New York, New York 10014

Published simultaneously in Canada
by McClelland & Stewart, Toronto

Editor: Virginia Buckley   Designer: Joseph Rutt
Printed in the U.S.A.   First Edition   10 9 8 7 6 5 4 3 2 1

**FRONTISPIECE: Typical men's and women's western wear in
the late 1940s**
Rockmount Ranch Wear

CONTENTS

Additional Photo Credits   vi

Acknowledgments   vii

1 Cowboys Past, Present, and Future   1

2 Hats   11

3 Shirts   27

4 Jeans   39

5 Boots   47

6 Accessories   61

Museums   71

Bibliography and Suggested Reading   73

Index   75

An eight-page color insert follows page 56.

ADDITIONAL PHOTO CREDITS

The following photographs are courtesy of the Erwin E. Smith Collection of the Library of Congress on deposit at the Amon Carter Museum, Fort Worth, Texas:

Page 3 LC S6-367, Erwin S. Smith: "Little Joe the Wrangler," n.d.

Page 13 LC S6-82, Erwin E. Smith: "Cowpunchers Sitting Around the Fire, Eating, SMS Range, Texas, 1908"

Page 28 LC S61-3, Erwin E. Smith: "Matador Outfit Eating at the Chuck Wagon, Matador Ranch, Texas, 1891"

Page 48 LC S6-221, Erwin E. Smith: "Harry Campbell Cleaning His Gun, Matador Ranch, Texas, 1908"

Page 64 LC S611-16 Erwin E. Smith: "A Small Group of Negro Cowboys with Their Mounts Saddled up Posed in Connection with a Fair in Bonham, Texas, in the Interest of Interracial Relations, circa 1909–1910"

ACKNOWLEDGMENTS

The joy of researching this book was meeting so many wonderful people who were willing to share their knowledge, stories, time, and artifacts with me. I would like to thank Richard Rattenbury, Curator of History at the National Cowboy Hall of Fame and Western Heritage Center in Oklahoma City, Oklahoma, who started me on the right track and verified my final manuscript; B. Byron Price, Executive Director of the National Cowboy Hall of Fame and Western Heritage Center; Albert H. Luiz, formerly Vice President Manufacturing, Resistol Hats, who provided information and a tour and read the chapter on hats; Jack A. Weil, Jack B. Weil, and Steven E. Weil of the Rockmount Ranch Wear Manfacturing Company, who told me their tales and confirmed the chapter on shirts; Lynn Downey, historian, and Dori Wofford of Levi Strauss & Company, who verified the chapter on jeans; H. Joe Justin, who shared his stories of the Justin family and validated the chapter on boots; Eddie Kelly, designer, Justin Boot Company; Mark and Lisa Foster, Foster's Western Wear and Saddle Shop, Denton, Texas; Kathy Bressler, Cattle Kate, Wilson, Wyoming; Kent Williams, Montana Silversmiths, Columbus, Montana; Ann Hall for the pun in the title; and all of the people who let me take their pictures.

Brothers serious about learning the trade at the Fort Worth Stock Show. Note the trophy belt buckles, tooled belts, snap-button shirts, and Roper boots.

M. Jean Greenlaw

1

COWBOYS PAST, PRESENT, AND FUTURE

Do you own a pair of blue jeans? Have you ever worn a snap-button western shirt, a cowboy hat, or a pair of western boots? If so, then you are a part of the most enduring fashion in clothing, generally known as western wear.

The first American cowboys were herding cattle in Texas by 1830, but it wasn't until 1867 that cowboys became legendary. That year, Joe McCoy bought most of the townsite of Abilene, Kansas, and advertised for cowboys to herd longhorn cattle up the Chisholm Trail from Texas, where they would be shipped by railroad to the East. These cowboys of the Chisholm Trail became famous in songs and newspaper stories, and many people thought the life of a cowboy was a wonderful adventure.

In fact, cowboys had a hard and dangerous life. Most cowboys were young, in their teens and twenties. They spent weeks out on the range eating beans and biscuits, were often in the saddle for eighteen hours, and then slept in a bedroll or tent on the hard ground, their saddle for a pillow. When they were at a ranch, their days lasted ten to fourteen hours, and they slept in a bunkhouse that wasn't much more comfortable than the open range. The main work of a cowboy was to tend cattle: roping, branding, herding, and seeing to their needs. Cowboys were restless, moving from ranch to ranch for work until they were too old or too injured to continue.

Many songs were created by cowboys and were sung to keep cattle from stampeding, as well as to make the nights less lonely. The songs were often sad ballads that told of the hard life the cowboy led. One song, written by N. Howard Thorp of Socorro, New Mexico, in 1898, tells of the fate of a young horse wrangler.

Branding at the L. S. Ranch, Tascosa, Texas, 1902
National Cowboy Hall of Fame Collection

"Little Joe the Wrangler" was a young Texas stray who left his family because he was beaten. The cowboys on a drive up the Chisholm Trail took pity on him and let him join them. At a camp on the Red River, a norther blew in and stampeded the cattle. All hands were called out, and, when the cattle were under control, one hand was missing.

Next morning just at sunup we found where Rocket fell,
Down in a washout twenty feet below;
Beneath his horse, mashed to a pulp, his spurs had rung the knell
For our little Texas stray—poor Wrangler Joe.

"Little Joe the Wrangler"
Erwin E. Smith Collection of the Library of Congress on deposit at the Amon Carter Museum

Life for a cowboy wasn't all work, however. At the end of the trail drive or once every several months, cowboys would go into town for entertainment and relaxation. This tended to be rather rowdy, as the frontier was a rough place, and the cowboys were among the roughest of the settlers.

In the more than one hundred and seventy years since the cowboy has been a part of the West, the life has changed to some extent. There are no more trail drives, and technology makes the work easier. Most cowboys have pickup trucks and can step out every Saturday night. Often, cowboys have a good education, and some have attended college to learn how to do the many things necessary in running a modern ranch.

Being a cowboy today involves the whole family. Go to a rodeo and you will see grandfathers passing on their way of life to a grandchild. Go to a stock show and you will see the young boys and girls who are the cowboys and ranchers of the future.

Some things have not changed. Cowboys are not about to give up their horses. There is a bond between the cowboy and his horse that is important, and the horse can also do many tasks on a ranch that a pickup can't. The cowboy still spends many hours outside in all kinds of weather, which takes its toll on the body, and there are dangers that must be faced on a daily basis.

Western wear has changed very slowly since its origins more than one hundred and twenty years ago. Right after the Civil War, in the late 1860s, many of the cowboys wore

Passing on the heritage
M. Jean Greenlaw

A man and his horse are a team.

M. Jean Greenlaw

castoffs from war uniforms. Not until the 1870s did the distinctive clothing known today as western wear begin. The most important features of clothing then and now are comfort, utility, quality, and style. Since a cowboy or cowgirl spends long hours working, the clothing must be comfortable whether the wearer is riding, sitting, kneeling, or standing. Certain pieces of clothing, like chaps and vests, developed from the special needs of the cowboy, and hard use made the cowboy demand only quality materials. Though the basic style of western wear remains the same, there were small changes that have come and gone over the years. The "urban cowboy" craze of the early 1980s had nothing to do with real cowboys and caused them a great deal of embarrassment.

People from all over the world enjoy wearing western clothes because of the comfort and style, making it a big business today. Large manufacturing companies, like Levi Strauss & Company, produce jeans and shirts in massive quantities, and smaller producers, like Rockmount Ranch Wear Manufacturing Company, create all manner of western wear, including snap-button western shirts and accessories such as bolo ties. There are also small specialty companies. Cattle Kate manufactures contemporary clothing with the frontier spirit and romance of the West, and Montana Silversmiths crafts silver belt buckles, scarf slides, bolos, and other accessories.

Western wear is sold in department stores, but it is far more interesting to go to a western wear store or thumb through specialty catalogs. It is amazing how many items are featured. Sheplers claims to have the world's largest

Ranching is family business, so girls and women are also involved.

M. Jean Greenlaw

western catalog, and their stores are huge. But single, family-owned stores, such as Foster's in Denton, Texas, also have numerous customers, including shoppers from many countries. Lisa Foster, the co-owner, says she can tell what kinds of clothes people will buy from their attire when they walk into the store. Many employees in both Foster's and Sheplers have worked in those stores all of

A proud prize winner at the Fort Worth Stock Show
M. Jean Greenlaw

their careers and love the work and the clothing they sell.

The history of western wear is peopled with pioneers, characters, entrepreneurs, and just plain good folks. Their stories are filled with the romance of the West and are testimonies to their good fortune in having the right ideas at the right time as well as the hard work it took to make a difference.

the last drop from his STETSON

"The Last Drop from His Stetson,"
the most famous of all western posters
John B. Stetson Company

2

HATS

For the wearer of western attire, the cowboy hat is the most important item of clothing and has been since the 1870s. Whether the wearer is a man or woman, boy or girl, the hat makes an important statement. From it, those in the know can sometimes tell if the wearer is a rancher or rodeo cowboy, and if the latter, whether a bull rider or roper. Any self-respecting cowboy or cowgirl owns six or more hats, buying a new one each year and rarely getting rid of the old ones. Felts and straws are worn according to preference, and both are part of the wardrobe.

The history of cowboy hats actually begins with a legend about a French monk in the sixteenth century who was making a pilgrimage. After traveling for some time, he became weary and hungry, and his shoes wore thin. While he was resting beside the road, a passing farmer took pity on him and gave him a rabbit. The monk skinned and cooked the animal, filling his empty stomach and gaining strength for the rest of the journey. Looking at the rabbit skin, the monk decided to stuff his worn shoes with the fur and continued on his way. After several days of walking in the summer heat, the monk noticed that the fur in his shoes had become a kind of cloth. The heat and perspiration from his body, combined with the constant rubbing of his feet, had caused the fur fibers to interlock.

Though the legend may not be true, the material known as felt was produced in the sixteenth century, and hatters realized that this cloth would make good headwear, as it shed rain and kept its shape. The same basic method of making hats has been used over the centuries, with one addition that proved fatal to some manufacturers and wearers. For a while, mercury, which is poisonous, was used in making hats. This caused some workers, as well as hat wearers, to become insane, which is where we get the term "mad as a hatter." Fortunately, mercury is no longer used in making hats.

The western hat as we know it today was invented by a Philadelphia hat maker named John B. Stetson. Becoming seriously ill with tuberculosis in 1860, he decided to go West where there were open skies and clean air. Stetson settled in St. Joseph, Missouri, and took up brick-making, but his business was washed away in a flood. Broke and horseless, Stetson joined a small band of men who set out on foot in 1862 to trek to the gold rush at Pike's Peak.

On the way, Stetson used his knowledge of felting to make a cover to protect himself and the men in his party from storms. He then made himself a crude high-crowned and wide-brimmed hat to shield him from the sun and rain.

Though Stetson's companions laughed at the hat, a passing bullwhacker, driving his yoke of oxen, bought it from him for a five-dollar gold piece. This was the first "John B. Stetson" hat ever made and sold.

Stetson did not gain wealth in the West, but he did regain his health. Deciding to return to Philadelphia, Stetson once again started a hat business. After struggling to make a living, he remembered the hat he had made while in the West and began a new line to be sold to westerners, which he named "The Boss of the Plains." The hat caught on immediately and soon became known as a "Stetson" or a "John B."

Notice the many styles of hats worn by these men.
Erwin E. Smith Collection of the Library of Congress on deposit at the Amon Carter Museum

The Stetson took on many shapes, as each cowboy and cowgirl molded the hat to suit his or her personality. Most riders decorated their hats with a band, which was both ornamental and useful for adjusting the size of the hat to fit the rider's head. Leather studded with conchas, rattlesnake skin, Indian beads, and woven horsehair all served as bands. Some riders also made bonnet strings to keep the hat from flying off in windy weather or when they were chasing cattle.

The western hat had numerous uses. The wide brim was a sunshade for a cowboy's eyes, allowing him to see great distances or, pulled down in the back, keeping his neck from burning in the hot sun. A hat served as an umbrella in the rain, with a rolled brim funneling the rain so it didn't pour down the cowboy's neck or into his eyes. The tall crown allowed air to circulate around the cowboy's head to cool him in the summer, and the brim, worn over the ears in winter, could protect a cowboy from frostbite.

A cowboy also used his hat for work. It came in mighty handy for controlling cattle and spurring on a horse. The Stetson could serve as a water bucket for horses, and for putting out a campfire or fighting a grass fire. A campfire, sometimes made of cow chips and slow to catch, could be fanned into life with a hat, and the same hat served as a pillow for a weary head. A cowboy could use a hat in his hand for balance while riding, the way a tightrope walker uses a pole, or he could signal others with it. Today, cowboys and cowgirls use their hats for many of the same purposes, and probably for others not mentioned here.

Women riders, with hats to fit their personalities, 1925
Photo R. R. Doubleday, National Cowboy Hall of Fame Collection

They also continue to personalize their headwear, choosing the crease and roll they like and adding decorations such as pins and other accessories. The western hat makes a personal statement about the wearer, but it also continues to serve as a useful tool.

Dating from 1880 to the present, these western hats illustrate
stylistic variations responding to regional tastes and
various interpretive influences.
TOP ROW, LEFT TO RIGHT: Texas pattern by Rekcud, 1880–1885;
Southwestern peak by Stetson, 1910–1915; custom crease
by Stetson, 1920–1925; and "ten-gallon" rodeo pattern
by Stetson, 1930–1935
BOTTOM ROW, LEFT TO RIGHT: oversized rodeo and show pattern
custom made by Resistol, 1940–1945; box crease by Stetson,
1950–1955; contemporary style by Eddy Brothers, 1965–1975;
"urban cowboy" and country music pattern by Charlie 1
Horse, 1980–1985; and contemporary dress pattern
by Resistol, 1989–1990
National Cowboy Hall of Fame Collection

Felt hats are made from Canadian beaver skins, rabbit skins that come from France, and skins of nutria, a South American rodent. The beaver that is used is mostly the trimmings of fur coats. Rabbits are a meat industry in France, but the skins are not used, so the hat industry buys them. The skins are cleaned, and the long hairs of the animals are cut off, leaving the downy under-fur. Only this under-fur has on the surface of each hair the barblike projections that will lock the fibers together to make a strong felt. The under-fur is treated in a chemical solution similar to that used in a home permanent, to make the fur fibers curl. When these fibers are later placed in hot water, they will form barbs that interlock in every direction.

The fur is sheared off the skins and cleaned by a method in which the fur is blown through a chamber. The desirable under-fur floats through the chamber, and the heavier debris and hair falls out and is discarded. The fur is bagged and sent to another cleaner. The beaver and rabbit furs are then blended in a mixer and weighed out one hat at a time—seven ounces in weight and about 28 inches by 36 inches in size. Felt hats are mostly made of rabbit fur, and the more beaver in the mix, the more expensive the hat will be. A buyer can tell how much beaver is in a hat by a number before the letter X. The standard hat is 4X, and the quality goes up to the top of the line. Blends of beaver, nutria, and exotic furs such as chinchilla and sable are used in hats of 100X quality and higher.

The blended fur is placed in a former, which is a large chamber with an exhaust fan at the bottom and a two-foot-high perforated cone over the source of the suction. Fur comes in at the top, rollers kick it up, and then the cloud of fur is sucked down on the cone, forming a thick mass as delicate as a blanket of dust.

A wet burlap blanket is carefully wrapped around the cone, and it is put in a sinker tub filled with hot water. When the hot water hits the fur, the fibers curl up and interlock like Velcro, which starts the felting process. The cone is removed from the water, and the fur is carefully stripped off the metal. Three to six hats are wrapped together in a blanket to start the shrinking process. The roll of hats is massaged to force the fibers together, making each hat harden and tighten. Each cone-shaped mass of fur shrinks to less than half its original size and gets very dense.

The resulting shapes are dyed, stiffened with shellac, and separated into basic sizes of small, medium, large, and extra large. The hats are then blocked to a specific size and style, and the crowns and brims are pressed, which starts the finishing process. A sharking wheel, called that because it is covered with sharkskin, is used to pull out any loose fibers, and the hat is steamed, singed, greased with hatter's oil, and pounced (like sanding a piece of furniture) several times. Powder is put on the hat to even out the color, and some of the hats are steamed into traditional shapes. Linings and sweatbands are inserted, and the final decorative trim is added. In all, there are two hundred operations, most of them done by hand, that go into making a western hat.

Stacks of hats waiting to be blocked and
styled at the Resistol plant

M. Jean Greenlaw

Blocking and pressing
M. Jean Greenlaw

Using a sharking wheel to remove loose fibers
M. Jean Greenlaw

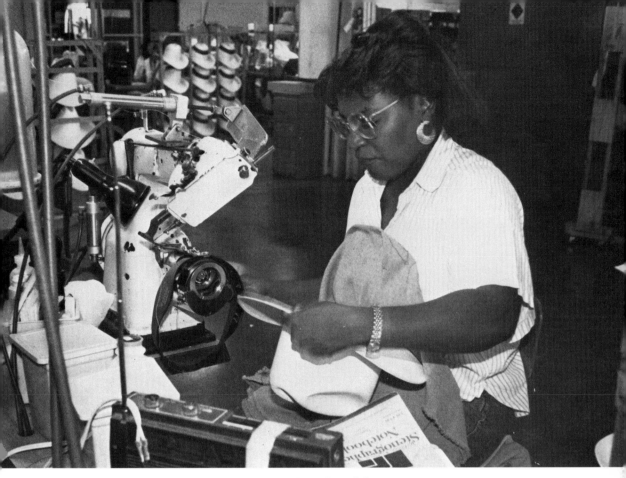

Adding the hatband and lining
M. Jean Greenlaw

Straw hats are made by a different process. The straw
bodies are woven as a cottage industry in China and
Ecuador. In China, they are woven of paper fiber, whereas
in Ecuador, they are woven of tequila palm. Men go out on
donkeys to cut the palm and boil the fronds. Fibers are then
stripped out by fingernail, dried, and taken by bus to the
village to be sold at market. Women buy the strands and
weave them into straw hat bodies, taking two days to two
months, depending on the quality of body they are making. The bodies, which are cone shaped, are taken back to
the market and sold to a collector who sizes, grades, and

Straw hat bodies as they arrive from Ecuador
M. Jean Greenlaw

bleaches them before sending them to the United States. The bodies arrive in rough form and are cleaned, bleached, and blocked. The brim is trimmed, and a wire is sewn in to help the hat keep its shape. The hat is then lacquered and pressed into shape, and a lining, sweatband, and trim are added.

Hats come in a variety of colors from deep black through many shades of gray to white; some hats are even brown. The colors have interesting names such as crystal, silver belly, sterling, and graphite. The width of the brim, the height of the crown, and the crease put in the hat are choices made by each buyer. Though some hats are creased at the factory, many are sent to western wear stores with an open crown so they can be shaped to the desires of the buyer.

Creasing a hat for a customer in Fort Worth
M. Jean Greenlaw

A rite of passage—getting his first cowboy hat!

M. Jean Greenlaw

There are standard creases known as cattleman, quarter horse, Texan, buckaroo, hondo, rodeo, and bull rider. Creases are also affected by movies and country-and-western singers. The television movie special *Lonesome Dove* brought back the Tom Mix crease and the four-inch brim. Singers George Strait and Garth Brooks each have a hat style and crease that is named for them. Fans are quick to choose these hats so they can identify with their favorite entertainers.

The John B. Stetson Company is no longer an independent hat maker. It has been bought by Resistol, which was founded in 1927 and is located in Garland, Texas. Resistol became known for the invention of the self-conforming hatband, which provides a comfortably cushioned fit. Resistol makes hats under both the Resistol and Stetson names. Resistols are for the working cowboy and Stetsons are for the brand conscious.

Today, there are many brands of hat to choose from, and getting that first hat is an important rite of passage. The western hat has undergone changes since 1865, but it is still recognizable and will probably continue in its basic form, as long as there is the West.

Steve Weil holding a shirt sold in 1948. Note the piping and the smile pocket.

Rockmount Ranch Wear

3

SHIRTS

In the early days of the cowboy, the shirt was the least important garment as far as style was concerned. Immediately following the Civil War, shirts often were castoffs from uniforms and were gray or blue. As these uniform shirts wore out, cowboys took to wearing collarless, starchless shirts, or anything they could get their hands on. They wore woolen shirts in winter and cotton in summer, usually four- or five-button pullovers that always had long sleeves for protection. Shirts came in checks, stripes, or solids, but colors were limited to the drab and dreary. Red was not acceptable because it was believed that the color disturbed the cattle.

Entertainers were the first to liven up the western shirt. Performers in Buffalo Bill Cody's Wild West Show, which he started in 1883, wore fringed buckskin shirts. Hollywood began making western films in the early 1900s, and Tom Mix chose to wear tailored shirts, some of which had but-

On these cowboys, heavy work shirts of many patterns and styles as well as a few vests can be seen.

Erwin E. Smith Collection of the Library of Congress on deposit at the Amon Carter Museum

toned bib fronts. John Wayne and the famous 1950s saddle bronc rider Casey Tibbs are the most notable wearers of the bib front shirt. These shirts have come in and out of fashion but are a staple in western wear today. Until the 1930s, however, the average cowhand still stuck with a variety of plain shirts.

Among the film entertainers of the 1930s, the singing cowboys Gene Autry and Roy Rogers wore costumes that were decorative and flashy. Rodeo was becoming popular, and rodeo cowboys wanted to distinguish themselves from the working cowboys, so their clothing became fancier. And last but not least, country-and-western performers wore elaborate costumes designed by the Los Angeles clothier Nudie.

Casey Tibbs in a snap-button bib shirt, 1950
National Cowboy Hall of Fame Collection

Any shirt that was warm and comfortable was appropriate, 1920.

Photo R. R. Doubleday, National Cowboy Hall of Fame Collection

The time was right for an entrepreneur like Jack A. Weil to establish fashions for the working cowhand that continue to this day. Weil came West with his wife in 1928, traveling on gravel roads to reach Denver, where he still lives. There, Weil set up a sales office for a Chicago-based firm, and he roamed the untamed West to such cities as El Paso, Texas, Great Falls, Montana, Boise, Idaho, Salt Lake City, Utah, and Phoenix, Arizona, selling women's garters

Mc Laughlin brothers, trick ropers, 1930s
Photo R. R. Doubleday, National Cowboy Hall of Fame Collection

and garments. Travel was difficult, but there was excitement in being part of the adventure of settling the raw but beautiful land.

One day in 1934, in the middle of the Depression, Jack A. Weil and his friend Phil Miller had lunch. Phil wanted Jack to go in business with him, but Jack liked his steady job. Jack did advise Miller that he would never make a lot of money if all he did was buy and sell; he had to produce as well. Phil replied that he had the money to start a business, if Jack would do the design and manufacturing. Jack agreed and became a partner in Miller and Company of Denver, which is now Miller Stockman.

The first thing they did was open up the Texas Rancher's Supply Company in Fort Worth, Texas. They did this in 1935 to take advantage of the Texas state centennial that was to take place the next year. The store stayed open three years and was the beginning of the development of western wear as a separate business. Even though it was the Depression, cowboys earned fifteen to twenty dollars a month with room and board, so their pay was clear. When they came into town every month or two, they wanted to raise a bit of a ruckus and to be dressed up for the occasion.

Young cowhands sought something colorful and flamboyant, so Weil produced cotton sateen shirts. He began with red, blue, green, and yellow shirts, but he couldn't sell the yellow ones because there is a superstition, particularly among the Navaho, that yellow is the sign of death. Plaids became popular, with blue and red being the favorite mix. Shirts sold for $1.69 to $2.00, a price that cowhands could afford.

In order to help develop a taste for western wear, Weil and Miller visited towns that had rodeos. Working through organizations like the Chamber of Commerce, Rotary Club, Elks, and Kiwanis, they established a city-wide tradition that anyone who didn't dress up in western wear during the rodeo could be fined by a kangaroo court or dunked in a horse trough!

Western shirts were designed to be fitted, which made the cowhand look trimmer and also served to keep the shirt from catching on saddle horns and barbed wire. Shirttails were long so they would stay tucked in while wearers were working or dancing. The shirts had a yoke across the shoulders, which helped the cowboy's shoulders look broader and also made the shirt more durable. The yoke was often outlined in piping or cording, to accent the width and to provide a bit of flash.

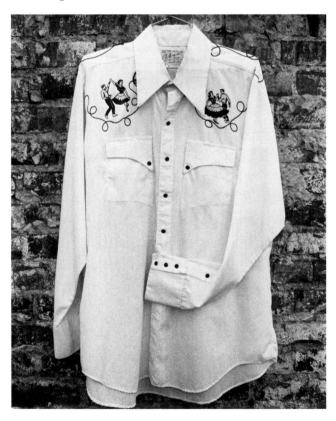

A square-dance shirt with piping and snap-button flap pockets, Rockmount Ranch Wear, 1955

M. Jean Greenlaw

Pockets in western shirts are of two types, the snapped flap pocket or one known as a smile or half-moon pattern. The flap pocket allowed the cowhand to keep things safely snapped in during riding and roping. The smile pocket was reinforced at the ends with decorative embroidery. Cuffs were made to fit tightly, so the shirt didn't slide over a cowboy's hands while he was working.

Jack A. Weil is most noted in the western wear business for creating the snap-button western shirt. In fact, his company uses the motto "We put the snap in western wear!" In 1938, Weil was in San Francisco, where he saw a Chinese tailor putting a mother-of-pearl snap on a dress shirt. It was beautiful, but not practical, because the pearl would break when put through a washing machine wringer or when hit with a hot iron. Weil decided that plain snaps that were rings of metal would be practical and serviceable. He came back to Denver, called the Scovill Manufacturing Company in Connecticut, and told them he wanted to put their Gripper Snap on western shirts. The snap company was reluctant to send the snaps because they thought it was an incorrect application. Weil persisted and put these simple ring fasteners on his shirts. He would have to wait until after World War II to perfect his use of the snaps, which are still popular today. One side benefit of a snap-button shirt is that if a cowboy is dragged or caught on a bull's horn, the shirt pops open for a timely escape.

In 1946, Weil began his own company, Rockmount Ranch Wear Manufacturing Company, because he wanted to focus on designing and manufacturing only the highest quality western wear, which he and his son, Jack B. Weil, and his grandson, Steve Weil, continue to do today. Though Jack A. Weil is in his nineties, he still opens up his office at 7:00 A.M. six days of the week. Every order is filled with a personal touch, and in many, a handwritten note is attached, continuing the tradition of individual service to customers.

**Jack A. Weil, Steve Weil, and Jack B. Weil,
three generations of western tradition**
M. Jean Greenlaw

The Rockmount Ranch Wear Manufacturing Company produces women's and children's clothes, as well as men's. In the 1950s, they also created matching outfits for an exhibition dance group that performed during intermissions across from the opera house in Central City, Colorado. These costumes became the accepted wear for square dancing and are still in vogue today. An interesting fact about these dance clothes was that, whereas the women's shirts had short sleeves, the men's shirts had long sleeves—so women didn't have to grab a sweaty arm!

**Square-dance costumes became fashionable in the 1950s.
Men's sleeves were long, women's short.**
M. Jean Greenlaw from a poster courtesy Rockmount Ranch Wear

Preparing to ride at the Fort Worth Stock Show
M. Jean Greenlaw

There are approximately eight companies making western shirts today. Styles and fabrics change, but the essence of the shirt remains. Whether one wants a shirt for looking one's best at a stock show, or for work, rodeo days, hanging out, or socializing on Saturday night, the selection is not only large but is instantly recognizable as western.

Showing off his Levi's
Levi Strauss & Company

4

JEANS

Can you imagine a world without jeans? Comfortable and durable as well as acceptable for almost any occasion, jeans can be worn with anything and are found all over the world. Jeans are popular not only in the United States; if an American traveler goes to another country, he or she is frequently asked to trade a pair of jeans for a variety of goods or a great amount of money.

The word "jeans" was actually used before Levi Strauss created his famous work pants. As with many stories passed down by word-of-mouth, the exact truth cannot be known, but the story is both engaging and plausible. A fabric woven in Genoa, Italy, for many centuries was used in pants for Italian sailors and was said to have been used to make the sails on Columbus's ships. The pants were long-wearing, and people from other countries began to want trousers made from this cloth. Over time, the word "Genoese," used to describe the pants, was shortened and changed to "jeans." Levi Strauss probably sold pants of this type when he was a peddler. The word "jeans" was not used in connection with Levi's pants for many years.

Where did this phenomenon known as Levi's jeans all begin? Levi Strauss arrived in New York City with his family in 1847, an immigrant from Germany. He and his

Levi Strauss
Levi Strauss & Company

40

brothers were peddlers, traveling around the state of New York, selling their wares, and bringing news to homes and villages. The dream of most peddlers was to become merchants, which is what the Strauss brothers accomplished. The gold rush in California began in 1849, and Levi Strauss's brother-in-law, David Stern, went West to set up a dry goods business in San Francisco. Levi Strauss followed him to join the business in 1853.

The gold rush in California was in full swing when Levi arrived in San Francisco on March 14, 1853. Levi had no intention of seeking gold in the hills; he planned to be a merchant and let the miners bring the gold to him. It is probable that Levi made a visit to the remote mining camps, taking some of his new company's dry goods along. Legend has it that a miner told him he should have brought pants instead, as the miners' clothing wore out quickly and a fortune in gold dust could be lost from a torn pocket. Whatever the truth is about how Levi got the idea, he did take some sturdy fabric to a tailor, who made up a pair of pants Levi called overalls, and the rest is history.

Levi Strauss and David Stern named their shop Levi Strauss & Company. Business continued to grow, and in 1866, Levi opened a four-story sales and manufacturing office. During this time, Levi began to carry a rugged cotton cloth called denim. This material was originally woven in Nîme, France, and termed serge de Nîme. When the cloth began to be manufactured in the United States, its name was shortened to denim. Levi Strauss bought his cloth from a manufacturer in New England, and chose indigo blue as the color for the material.

Miners all over California were wearing Levi's overalls, which were finally given the lot number 501 in 1890. These overalls weren't known as jeans until 1960. The 501 jeans are still a big seller today. The original pants were made from shrink-to-fit denim, so the miners and cowboys who wore them would usually jump in a creek or a horse trough to shrink the jeans to the proper size.

Refinements were still being made to the denim pants. In Reno, Nevada, a tailor named Jacob Davis wrote to Levi Strauss in 1872. He had been adding copper rivets to the

Miners in their Levi pants
Levi Strauss & Company

corners of the pockets of the denim jeans, making them much stronger. He offered to share the patent with Strauss, if his company would apply for it. A patent was assigned to Davis and to Levi Strauss & Company on May 20, 1873, and with the added durability, jeans became even more popular in the West.

Orange stitching was used on the pants to match the copper rivets. On the back pants pockets, a double row of stitches was sewn in the shape of curving V's. This design was added in 1873, and though it was not registered as a trademark until 1943, it is the oldest clothing trademark still in use. In 1886, a leather label was added to the waistband at the rear, and in 1936, the red tab was added to the right back pocket of the 501s. In 1937, the copper rivets were concealed on the rear pockets because they scratched the surface of anything the wearer sat on, from saddles to school desks!

The Levi's overalls were the favorite of Westerners for decades, but they were little known in the East until the Depression in the 1930s. Ranches in the West were trying to keep from going bankrupt, so they started what became known as dude ranches. The Easterners who came to enjoy the adventure of a western vacation soon discovered Levi's overalls and bought them to wear and then take home. "Lady Levi's" also became popular. As more people learned about them, Levi's overalls began to be a national product.

Though World War II slowed production of all goods, the boom after the war caused Levi Strauss & Company to expand its line beyond denim overalls and jackets. The 557

Poster advertising Levi overalls
Levi Strauss & Company

cowboy jean is popular because it is cut fuller. It is possible to buy Levi's 501 jeans that are preshrunk (no more jumping in horse troughs) and are available in several colors and finishes. Levi's shirts are also in demand. A recent poll conducted by a news magazine reports that, when it comes to blue jeans, Levi's 501 jeans are ranked first by a wide margin among all age groups. More than two billion pairs of Levi's 501 jeans have been sold since the pants were first designed in 1853!

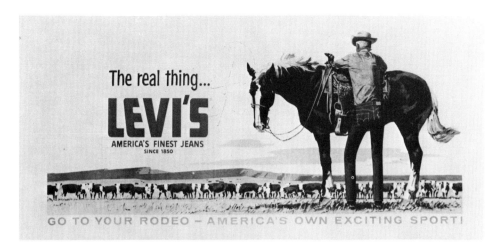

The real thing...

LEVI'S

AMERICA'S FINEST JEANS
SINCE 1850

GO TO YOUR RODEO – AMERICA'S OWN EXCITING SPORT!

**Levi's trademark stitching, pocket pattern, and leather label
are easily seen.**
Levi Strauss & Company

Other companies also produce jeans. For instance, the V. F. Corporation has two divisions, Lee and Wrangler, that manufacture jeans. Lee made their first cowboy jeans in about 1920, and Wrangler created their western-cut jeans in 1947. To assure the production of a jean that would be popular with cowboys, Wrangler sought the advice of rodeo cowboys. The resulting jeans had soft rivets that didn't scratch a saddle, cowboy-cut legs that fit over boots, and a raised pocket that allowed the cowboy to reach into it without getting off his horse. Wrangler is an official sponsor of the Professional Rodeo Cowboys Association and claims that 97 percent of rodeo cowboys wear their jeans.

No matter what brand of jeans you wear, you can be sure that you are in good company. Presidents, business men and women, students, and vacationers, to say nothing of cowboys, all have a pair or more, either on them or in the closet.

"VIVA!
EL CAMPEON"
(HURRAH! THE CHAMPION)

JUSTIN
BOOTS & SHOES

H. J. JUSTIN & SONS, INC. "BOOTMAKERS OF THE WEST SINCE 1879" FORT WORTH, TEXAS

The cover of the 1947 catalog of H. J. Justin & Sons, Inc.,
featured the narrow squared toe.

Justin Boot Company

5

BOOTS

The cowboy's boots were as important to him as his Stetson, and they were the most expensive part of his wardrobe. He often spent two months' wages for his boots and was very vain about them. It has been suggested that cowboys had small feet because they spent so much time in the saddle that their feet never spread. In the 1920s, Justin boots ranged from size four to nine, and eight and nine were considered large. Today, Justin boot sizes begin at eight and range to size eighteen, quite a sizeable difference!

As with other items of the cowboy's attire, the first boots on the range often were castoff uniform boots from the Civil War. The true cowboy boot began with the Coffeyville pattern, developed in the late 1860s. It was made in Coffeyville, Kansas, and was a combination of the American cavalry type and the British Wellington. There have been changes in cowboy boots over the years, but the basic style was set by the early 1900s.

**This cowboy is so proud of his boots that he pulled his pants
leg up to show them off for the camera.**

*Erwin Smith Collection of the Library of Congress on deposit at the
Amon Carter Museum*

The first cowboy boots were tall, many coming almost to
the knee. This was important because the boots served as
protection for the cowboy's legs as he was riding. When
chasing a steer, a cowboy couldn't pay attention to thorny
mesquite or other brush that would slap his legs. Stones
and other trash would fly up, and if the cowboy had on
short boots, they would soon be filled with debris and be
very uncomfortable. The stirrup would rub against the
cowboy's leg causing severe chafing, which was prevented
with a good pair of boots. When a cowboy was on the
ground, which he tried to avoid, there were rattlesnakes
and spiders he needed to be protected from.

Not only were the boots tall, they were tight. A cowboy
wanted a good fit so he didn't have to worry about his

balance while in the saddle. He also wanted them tight because he was vain about his small feet and wanted them to be shown off. These tall, tight boots were difficult to pull on, so they frequently had long straps called mule-ears sewn on to give the cowboy something to hang onto and tug. To keep the tall boots from flopping over or bunching up around the ankles, patterns of stitches were sewn into the upper leather of the boot to stiffen them. As the boot evolved, the stitching became more and more decorative;

TOP ROW, LEFT TO RIGHT: Coffeyville pattern, 1870–1875; stovepipe pattern, 1875–1890; early scallop-top cowboy pattern, 1910–1920; fancy dress pattern by Western Boot Company, 1920–1930; and inlaid "Texan" by Nocona, 1930–1940
BOTTOM ROW, LEFT TO RIGHT: fancy butterfly pattern by Nocona, 1940–1950; inlaid dress pattern with stovepipe tops by Olsen Stelzer, 1950–1960; custom-made dress pattern by Acme, 1960–1970; flashy bicentennial pattern by Tony Lama, 1976; and handcrafted, two-piece Torrejo pattern by
D.W. Frommer II
National Cowboy Hall of Fame Collection

colored threads and eventually insets and overlays were added to form designs. H. J. Justin is given credit for being the first to put decorative stitching on the uppers of boots. The stitching on the toe of the boot helped to make the cowboy's foot look smaller, but even more important, it kept the lining of the boot tight against the leather so the lining did not bunch up and become uncomfortable.

When chaps became popular, providing protection for a cowboy, boots gradually became shorter. The stovepipe or straight top of the boot became a decorative scallop of varying depths, adding to the attractiveness of the boot. Because the boot was shorter, the pull straps became much shorter, and now they are frequently a part of the decoration of the boot.

Boot heels have gone through varying styles since 1870. On the first Coffeyville and stovepipe boots, the heels were the width of the boot and relatively short and flat. By the 1900s, however, the boot heel had become two inches high, narrow, and extremely underslung. The country-and-western song "These Boots Were Made for Walking" did not describe the high-heeled underslung boots, as they were quite uncomfortable to walk in. In fact, it has been recorded that if a cowboy were thrown from his horse and had to walk home, he took his boots off to do the walking.

The tall, narrow boot heel was very good for riding, which is what a cowboy did most of the time. The thing a cowboy feared most was being thrown from his horse, "hung-up" by his boot, and dragged to death. This was the cause of many deaths on the range. The underslung boot heel gave the cowboy the best chance of shaking loose of the stirrup. Another benefit was that the high heel allowed

Lonna Trukey, champion relay and bronco rider, Pendelton, Oregon, 1919. An example of the deeply scalloped decorative boot.
National Cowboy Hall of Fame Collection

the cowboy to slide his foot through the stirrup until the heel rested against it. His weight could then be put on the arch of the foot, rather than the ball, which was more comfortable for hours in the saddle.

Over time, the 2-inch extreme underslung heel has been changed to a 1½-inch or 1¾-inch modified underslung. Some heels are tall and straight and are called stacked heels. Fashion stacked heels are the tallest of the cowboy boot heels. A utility heel gives height but is only slightly underslung. Because cowboys walk a good bit today, their boots sometimes have flat heels, as in the very popular Roper boot.

The popular Roper boot by Justin
Justin Boot Company

The toe of the cowboy boot began as either wide squared or rounded. This provided comfort as well as stability. As boots became more decorative, the pointed toe came into fashion. This point allowed the cowboy to slide his boot in and out of a stirrup easily, and it contributed to making his foot look small. However, there was not much room in the boot for toes, so comfort gave way to fashion. Through the years, every style of toe has been used in boots. Rounded, pointed, squared, and even wing-tipped have been worn.

When the western boot was first made in the 1870s, the material was hide from either a cow or a mule. Today, almost any type of skin is used in boots. Take your pick of cowhide, calfskin, painted python, pigskin, lizard, shark, buffalo, or snakeskin. You can get "hair-on" mink or kangaroo boots. Alligator is the most exotic, but not very practical, as the hide tends to split along the scales. Ostrich is a great favorite because of the comfort and durability, and ostriches are now being raised in the western United States for their hides. Boots are embroidered, and designs are inset or inlaid with various hides. Variety in embellishment and materials has certainly become the standard in western boots.

Boot makers of the Old West worked independently, making each pair of boots for a specific customer and sometimes taking months to do it. The boots were expensive, but a cowboy was willing to pay the price and generally stayed for life with a boot maker who had learned to fit him accurately. About six months before a cowboy reckoned he needed a new pair, he would place an order, to be sure he had them when he no longer was willing to be seen in his old boots.

There are still individuals and small companies making boots to special order. The Florentino Boot Company in Justin, Texas, consists of a husband and wife. Florentino Rodriguez makes the boots, and his wife, Susan, is the salesperson. Rodriguez is sought out by many who love boots because no two pairs are ever alike and the buyer can have a say in every aspect of the design. Paul Bond of Nogales, Arizona, is a former bronc rider, who, with twenty employees, turns out about twelve hundred pairs of custom-made boots a year. But most of the business of boot making is now done on a large scale.

The Justin boot is known as the "Standard of the West." Justin was the first to produce boots commercially, and they are still a major force in the market. H. Joe Justin, grandson of H. J. Justin, the founder of the Justin Boot Company, recently shared some memories of his family and the boot business.

H. J. "Joe" Justin left his home in Lafayette, Indiana, in 1879. He was only twenty years old, but his sense of adventure led him to Texas. The train took him as far as Gainesville, the end of the line in those days. Joe wanted to get to Spanish Fort, so he asked a mule skinner if he would take him there in his freight wagon. The mule skinner agreed, and when they arrived, Joe asked how much he owed. "How much do you have?" asked the mule skinner. "Five dollars and twenty-five cents," answered Joe. "Then give me five dollars. You'll need some money to get by on." The twenty-five cents were paper bills known as shin plasters and are on display at the Justin factory in Fort Worth.

Though he had some experience as a cobbler, Joe first found work in a barbershop. Spanish Fort was near the Red River crossing of the Chisholm Trail. When the cowboys came through on the trail, they bedded the cattle down before crossing the river, and then they came into town for a little excitement. One of the cowboys, O. C. Cato, asked Joe if he could make him a pair of boots. Joe agreed, but said it would take him some time to get them done. Cato replied, "O.K. I'm on my way to Dodge City, and I'll get them on my way back."

On another trip, Cato stopped by and said that if Joe could devise a way of taking a cowboy's foot measurement, Cato could sell boots for him. Joe designed a paper for tracing the foot and a tape for accurate measurement of the ball of the foot and the heel. This kit was responsible for the growth of Justin's reputation and business.

The railroad came to Nocona, Texas, in 1888, and the Justins (Joe was now married) moved to Nocona to make shipping easier. His business was booming, so he set up a shop and, a few years later, an even larger shop. Joe was a hard worker. He got up each morning at 4:00 A.M. and went down to the shop to start working. When his wife, Annie,

The interior of Justin's Nocona boot shop in 1912
Justin Boot Company

had breakfast ready, she would light a kerosene lamp and put it in the window, and Joe would come home for breakfast. You can see that kerosene lamp on display at the National Cowboy Hall of Fame and Western Heritage Center in Oklahoma City, where it is on loan from Joe's grandson, H. Joe Justin.

Joe and Annie had seven children: John, Anis, Fern, Earl, Enid, Sam, and Myrl. All of his sons would go into the boot business, as did Enid, who started her own company. In 1908, Joe took his sons into the business and changed the name of the company to H. J. Justin & Sons, Inc. In 1918, Joe died, and in 1925, John, Earl, and Sam moved the business to Fort Worth, where it still is today.

Enid Justin was not pleased with her brothers' move, so she stayed in Nocona and borrowed money to begin her own company, the Nocona Boot Company, which was very successful. Enid married twice, and after each divorce, her former husband opened up a boot company. This led one of Enid's brothers to suggest that she quit marrying, as she kept causing all of them more competition in the boot business!

The Depression of the 1930s saw the beginning of dude ranches, which attracted visitors from different areas, and western wear began to be popular in other parts of the United States. Before the 1930s, women either had their boots made by hand or they bought small men's sizes. Seeing a market, Justin constructed a women's boot last in 1934, and his company began manufacturing boots for women. The boot was known as the Western Gypsy and could be bought with a narrow squared toe or a rounded toe.

Levi's take many forms today.
Levi Strauss & Company

Silver is the accepted jewelry for western apparel.

Montana Silversmiths, Columbus, Montana

Jeans of all colors and sizes
M. Jean Greenlaw

Ropers come in many colors for the fashion conscious.
Justin Boot Company

Making a hand-tooled belt

M. Jean Greenlaw

Getting a Tom Mix crease in a new hat

M. Jean Greenlaw

Practice makes perfect at the rodeo.

Gary Goldberg, Wichita Falls, Texas

Colorful chaps for function and fashion
Gary Goldberg, Wichita Falls, Texas

Used Levi's are in popular demand.
M. Jean Greenlaw

Future rodeo stars
Gary Goldberg, Wichita Falls, Texas

Women's boots are commercially produced.
Justin Boot Company

Sam Justin had acquired much of the stock of the company, and he sold it to John Justin, Jr., in 1951. The company merged with Acme Brick and several other enterprises, and a few years later evolved into Justin Industries, Inc. Sam's son, Joe, went to work with Enid Justin in 1954. A salty lady, she was known to be "tougher than a boot." If the weather was bad and she couldn't drive to work, she would get out and walk through ice or snow. In 1974, her health began to fail, and in 1981, she merged her company with Justin's. Justin Industries now owns Justin, Nocona, and Tony Lama, the tops in boot making in the country. This company that began in 1879 still has a Justin at the head; John S. Justin, Jr., is Chairman of the Board and Chief Executive Officer.

The boot that took months to make by one person in 1879 still is made with great care. Miss Eddie Kelly, a boot designer with Justin since 1947, shared the information that it takes three weeks to make a pair of Justin boots. There are two hundred steps in making a boot and one hundred fifty people handle each boot. Eighteen hundred pairs of boots a day are completed in the Fort Worth factory, and approximately one million five hundred thousand pairs of boots are made a year. Boots are shipped to countries like Germany, Italy, and Japan, as well as throughout the United States.

Rows and rows of boots of all styles
M. Jean Greenlaw

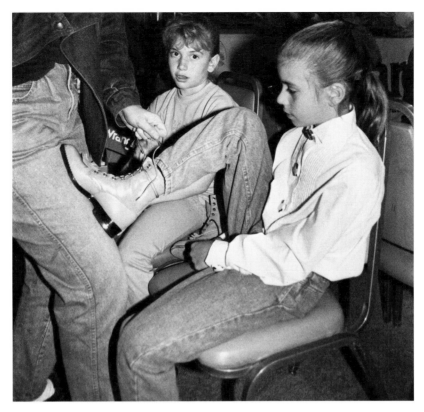

Trying on a pair of lace-up Ropers with a kiltie
M. Jean Greenlaw

When you go to a western wear shop today, you will find rows of boots awaiting your choice. You can choose round or pointed toes, short or high heels, short or tall length uppers, scalloped or stovepipe tops, and just about any skin imaginable. The most popular boot being sold today is the lace-up Roper. It has a flat heel, a round toe, and a removable fringed tongue called a kiltie. Women and men, girls and boys all like this boot. And if you don't see anything you like, ask around and you can find a boot maker who will make your boots to order.

**A bolo tie complements this ladies' attire
of the 1930s and 1940s.**

National Cowboy Hall of Fame Collection

6

ACCESSORIES

A cowboy owned very little that was not useful in his work. He lived in a bunkhouse that offered little privacy or space for storage, and he spent much of his time on the range, working cattle or mending fences. What he did own he decorated so that the useful became ornamental.

Chaps (pronounced "shaps") began to be popular in the mid 1870s and are still worn today. The word comes from the Spanish *chaparejos*, which means leather breeches or overalls. Chaps are a spin-off from the Mexican cowboy's *armas* or "leg armor," and they protected the cowboy's legs from brush, the thorns of the mesquite, and the bites of an ornery horse. They also provided warmth and covering from bad weather.

There are three kinds of chaps. Cowboys in Texas began wearing shotgun chaps in about 1870. They got this name because they looked like a double-barreled shotgun. These were close-fitting leather leggings that covered the

LEFT TO RIGHT: leather shotgun chaps; fringed shotgun chaps;
batwing chaps with conchas and brass studding made by
R. T. Frazier Saddlery, Pueblo, Colorado, circa 1905; woolies
National Cowboy Hall of Fame Collection

legs and buckled at the waist, leaving the rear open. Some
were plain leather, some were fringed, and the sides were
sewn shut. In order to put shotgun chaps on, a cowboy
would have to remove his spurs. In California, cowboys
were known as buckaroos, and they modified the shotgun
chaps by having them only long enough to cover from hip
to knee. The shorter chaps were known as "chinks."

Cowboys who lived in the cold northern plains of Montana and Wyoming preferred a version of the shotgun
chaps that was covered with fur or wool. These chaps,
called woolies, were most frequently covered with angora
goat hair, though other animal hides were also used. Cowboys in the Southwest did not wear woolies, as there was
too much brush that could catch in the hair.

In the early 1900s, the batwing chaps first appeared in

the eastern Rocky Mountains. Similar to a wide leather apron in the front, they buckled snugly around the leg in the back and were often decorated with silver conchas. Cowboys liked the batwings because they didn't have to remove their spurs to put them on and because these chaps were easy to get out of when a cowboy needed to do some work on the ground. Rodeo riders quickly adopted batwings, as the flapping chaps made their rides look even more exciting. Whether at work or socializing, cowboys wore their chaps.

A cowboy could not get into his pockets while riding, and rarely kept anything there anyway since it would make his ride uncomfortable. Cowboys seldom wore coats, which got in the way and could be dangerous; arms and legs had to be free for roping and riding. Therefore, the vest was a critical piece of clothing. Made of calfhide or store-bought wool, it provided warmth when buttoned up and, if left open, allowed the cowboy to stay cool. Most of all, it provided the cowboy with pockets. Among the things tucked into those pockets were a tobacco pouch, cigarette papers, matches, a tally sheet and pencil, and if the wearer was prosperous, a watch.

Some cowboys wore deerskin or elkhide gloves for warmth or to protect their hands while roping. These gloves were called gauntlets and had wide cuffs that came far up the arm. The military started the fashion, and Buffalo Bill Cody popularized it with his Wild West Show. Gauntlets were beautifully decorated with bead work, fringe, and embroidery. Some cowboys chose to wear leather cuffs instead of gloves, and these were also highly decorated.

The bandanna was commonly known as a wipe and sometimes called a rag or a wild rag. The first wipes were of cotton and were usually red, but sometimes blue or black. They were folded into a triangle and tied around the neck with a square knot. Generally the wipe was worn with the knot at the back, but if the sun got too hot on a cowboy's neck, the wipe was reversed. Riding herd was often dusty, so the wipe was pulled up over the nose as protection. It also served to protect from sleet or cold and could be tied over the ears to prevent frostbite. Wipes were used as towels after washing or to wipe perspiration from

These cowboys are wearing traditional wipes.
Erwin E. Smith Collection of the Library of Congress on deposit at the
Amon Carter Museum

a sweaty face. They could be a sling for a broken arm, a strainer for muddy water, a hot pad for a coffee pot or branding iron, a blindfold to lead a spooked horse, or a muzzle for a biting horse. The uses are endless.

Rodeo cowboys and cowgirls began to wear silk bandannas as part of their bright costumes. Cowboys today will wear cotton wipes for work, but when dressed to go to the Fort Worth Stockyards for a Saturday afternoon or dancing on a Saturday night, they will most likely wear a silk wipe.

An imported Spanish silk scarf finishes off this outfit featuring a ten-gallon nutria felt hat, a red suede vest, and split riding skirt trimmed with white leather fringe.
National Cowboy Hall of Fame Collection

The proper attire for a Saturday afternoon at the Fort Worth
Stockyards: a silk wipe, tooled leather belt with silver buckle
and tip, pressed and stacked jeans, and lace-up Ropers
M. Jean Greenlaw

A cowboy wearing skintight jeans had no use for a belt
to hold up his pants. It was in the 1930s, when rodeos
became popular, that belts and buckles were added to the
cowboys' and cowgirls' wardrobe. There had to be some
kind of trophy when an event was won. Most of the compet-
itors had no use for statues or plaques, so the trophy buckle
was created. The winner wore this buckle proudly, which
meant that belts became necessary. Belts were tooled by

A young man with a big trophy buckle
M. Jean Greenlaw

hand, with floral designs, geometric patterns, and silver conchas. Some cowboys had their names tooled in the leather at the back. The large trophy buckle is still fashionable, and you don't even have to win a rodeo contest to have one. Silversmiths make trophy buckles in many designs, with some being advertisements for a ranch.

John Justin, Jr., began manufacturing belts in 1938 from the scraps of boots made in his father's plant. He formed a company, the Justin-Barton Belt Company. When Mr. Barton retired, John bought him out and changed the name to the Justin Belt Company. Justin Industries still manufactures leather belts for the western trade. Today it is very hard to find a handmade belt, but there are some who do this work as a labor of love.

Jewelry was seldom worn by cowboys, until rodeos became a major part of western life. Most of the jewelry worn today is silver, because of the southwestern influence. Belt buckles and tips, tiaras for rodeo queens, earrings and button covers, conchas on belts and saddles—all are made of silver. Because cowboys and cowgirls believe in comfort as well as style, the bolo tie has gained favor. Whether the neck of a shirt is left open or closed, the wearer still looks fashionably dressed. The bolo is a braided leather thong that has silver tips and a decorative slide. Native Americans of the southwest created these ties, but they were first produced commercially by Rockmount Ranch Wear Manufacturing Company.

An accessory that is liked by some cowboys today is the duster. Though working cowboys rarely wear long coats because they get in the way when riding and roping, the duster is fine for going to a rodeo or a stock show.

Accessories are the finishing touches of any western outfit. They allow the wearer to express individuality while still being fashionably dressed in accepted western wear style. The authentic westerner knows how much is enough. The drugstore cowboy or urban cowboy often doesn't!

Western wear can be found almost anywhere in the world. The comfort, durability, and style appeal to many people, who go to great lengths to dress in western fash-

**Dressed for the annual Fort Worth Stock Show, this boy
is wearing a traditional wipe, a tooled belt, Roper boots,
and a duster.**

M. Jean Greenlaw

ion. This fashion has endured for more than one hundred
years, and it is possible to envision colonizers of Mars
dressed in western wear far into the next century!

MUSEUMS

The museums listed here are ones that specialize in western culture. A variety of artifacts can be found in each museum, and each of them has western clothing, either as apparel or in paintings and photographs.

Amon Carter Museum of Western Art
3501 Camp Bowie Blvd.
Fort Worth, Texas 76107

Black American West Museum and Heritage Center
3091 California St.
Denver, Colorado 80205

Boot Hill Museum
Front St.
Dodge City, Kansas 67801

Buffalo Bill Cody Memorial Museum
Rte. 5, P.O. Box 950
Golden, Colorado 80401

Buffalo Bill Historical Center
720 Sheridan Ave.
Cody, Wyoming 82414

Cattleman's Museum
1301 West 7th St.
Fort Worth, Texas 76102

Chisholm Trail Museum
605 Zellers Ave.
Kingfisher, Oklahoma 73750

Gene Autry Western Heritage Museum
5858 Sunset Blvd.
Box 710
Los Angeles, California 20078

Heart of Texas Historical Museum
117 High St.
Brady, Texas 76858

Lea County Cowboy Hall of Fame and Western Heritage Center
5317 Lobington Way
Hobbs, New Mexico 88240

The Museum
Texas Tech University
4th St. and Indiana Ave.
Lubbock, Texas 79409

Museum of the Big Bend
Sul Ross State University
U.S. 90 Entrance
Alpine, Texas 79830

**National Cowboy Hall of Fame
and Western Heritage Center**
1700 N.E. 63rd St.
Oklahoma City, Oklahoma 73111

**National Cowgirl Hall of Fame
and Western Heritage Center**
515 Ave. B
P.O. Box 1742
Hereford, Texas 79045

**North Fort Worth Historical
Society Museum**
Livestock Exchange Building
131 East Exchange
Fort Worth, Texas 76106

**Panhandle-Plains Historical
Museum**
2401 4th Ave.
Canyon, Texas 79016

Pawnee Bill Museum
P.O. Box 493
Pawnee, Oklahoma 74058

**Prorodeo Hall of Champions and
Museum of the American
Cowboy**
101 Pro Rodeo Dr.
Colorado Springs, Colorado 80919

**Sid Richardson Collection of
Western Art**
309 Main St.
Fort Worth, Texas 76102

**Texas Ranger Hall of Fame and
Museum**
Fort Fischer Park
P.O. Box 1370
Waco, Texas 76703

Tom Mix Museum
721 North Delaware
Dewey, Oklahoma 74029

**Tri State Old-Time Cowboys
Memorial Museum**
P.O. Box 202
Gordon, Nebraska 69343

Will Rogers Memorial
1720 West Will Rogers Blvd.
P.O. Box 157
Claremore, Oklahoma 74018

Woolaroc
Rte. 3
Bartlesville, Oklahoma 74003

BIBLIOGRAPHY AND SUGGESTED READING

Adams, Ramon F. *The Old-Time Cowhand.* Illustrated by Nick Eggenhofer. New York: Macmillan, 1961.

Christian, Mary Blount. *Hats Off to John Stetson.* Illustrated by Ib Ohlsson. New York: Macmillan, 1992.

Forbis, William H. *The Cowboys.* Alexandria, Va.: Time-Life Books, 1973.

Freedman, Russell. *Cowboys of the Wild West.* New York: Clarion, 1985.

Henry, Sandra, and Emily Taitz. *Everyone Wears His Name: A Biography of Levi Strauss.* Minneapolis: Dillon Press, 1990.

Kauffman, Sandra. *The Cowboy Catalog.* New York: Clarkson N. Potter, 1981.

"Levi's: An American Classic." *The Western Horseman* 54 (May 1989).

Lightfoot, D. J. *Trail Fever: The Life of a Texas Cowboy.* Illustrated by John Bobbish. New York: Lothrop, 1992.

Lomax, John A. *Cowboy Songs and Other Frontier Ballads.* New York: Macmillan, 1938.

Pattie, Jane. "Justin Boot: Standard of the West." *The Quarter Horse Journal* 40 (November 1987).

Rattenbury, Richard. Color photos by Ed Muno. "Western Fashion." *Persimmon Hill* 17 (Autumn 1989).

Richmond, Ralph. *The Stetson Century*. Philadelphia: John B. Stetson Company, 1965.

Rollins, Philip Ashton. *The Cowboy*. New York: Charles Scribner's Sons, 1922.

Taylor, Lonn, and Ingrid Maar. *The American Cowboy*. Washington, D.C.: American Folklife Center, 1983.

Tinkelman, Murray. *Rodeo*. New York: Greenwillow, 1982.

Van Steenwyk, Elizabeth. *Levi Strauss: The Blue Jeans Man*. New York: Walker & Co., 1988.

Weidt, Maryann. *My Blue Jeans: A Story About Levi Strauss*. Minneapolis: Carolrhoda, 1990.

Whitehead, Lea. "A History of Western Wear Fashion." *The Quarter Horse Journal* 42 (September 1989).

Wolf, Bernard. *Cowboy*. New York: Morrow, 1985.

INDEX

Page numbers in *italics* refer to illustrations.
References to color inserts are indicated by *ci*.

Abilene, Kansas, 1
Acme Brick, 57
Autry, Gene, 28

bandannas, *8, 10, 15, 29, 30, 48,* 64–65, *64, 65, 66, 69*
belt buckles:
  origin of, 66–67
  standard silver, 7, *35, 66*
  trophy, *ii, viii, 9, 23, 35, 37,* 66–67, *67, ci2*
belts:
  concha, *ii*
  manufacturing of, 66–68
  tooled, *ii, viii, 9, 23, 35,* 66–67, *66, 69, ci5*
bolo ties, 7, *26, 35, 60,* 68
"Boss of the Plains," 13
Boise, Idaho, 30
Bond, Paul, 53
boots:
  Coffeyville, 47, *49,* 50
  heel on, *49,* 50–51, *52,* 59
  height of, 48–50, *49,* 59
  insets and overlays on, *46, 49, 50, 57, 60*
  kiltie on, 59, *59, ci4*
  materials for, 53
  mule-ears on, 49–50, *49, 52, 57*
  scallops on, *15, 46, 49, 51, 57,* 59, *60*
  size of, 47–49, 55
  stitching on, *46, 49,* 49–50, *51,* 53, *57, 60*
  stovepipe, *48, 49,* 50, 59
  toe of, *49, 52, 52,* 56, 59
  use for, 48
  women's, 56, *57, 60*
  see also Justin boots, Ropers
branding, 2, *2*
Brooks, Garth, 25
buckaroos, 62
Buffalo Bill Cody's Wild West Show, 27, 63

California, 41, 62
Cato, O. C., 54–55
Cattle Kate, 7
Central City, Colorado, 36
Chamber of Commerce, 32
chaps:
  batwing, 62–63, *62, ci7*
  discussion of, 7, 50, 61–63
  shotgun, *10,* 61–62, *62*
  woolies, 62, *62*
Chicago, Illinois, 30
China, 21
Chisholm Trail, 1, 3, 54
Civil War, 4, 27, 47
clothing trademark, 43
Cody, Buffalo Bill, 63
Coffeyville, Kansas, 47
Columbus, 39
conchas, *ii,* 14, *62,* 68, *ci5*
Connecticut, 34
country-and-western performers, 25, 28
cowboys:
  bond with horse, 4, 6, *10*
  life of, 1–4, *2, 3, 5, 6,* 7, *13,* 14, 27, *28,* 32, 34, 47, *48,* 48–53, 61–68, *64*
creasing, *see* hat; shape of

Davis, Jacob, 42–43
denim, *see* Levi's
Denton, Texas, 8
Denver, Colorado, 30, 32, 34
Depression, 31–32, 43, 56
Dodge City, Kansas, 54
dude ranches, 43, 56
duster, 68, *69*

Ecuador, 21
Elks, 32
El Paso, Texas, 30

felting:
    legend of, 11–12
    process of, 11–12, 17–18
film stars, 25, 27–28, *ci5*
Florentino Boot Company, 53
Fort Worth Stock Show, *viii*, *9*,
    37, *69*
Fort Worth Stockyards, 65, *66*
Fort Worth, Texas, *viii*, *9*, 32, 54,
    56, 58, 65, *66*, *69*
Foster, Lisa, 8
Foster's, 8
future generations, *viii*, *4*, *5*, *8*,
    9, *24*, *35*, 67, *69*, *ci6*, *ci8*

Gainesville, Texas, 54
Garland, Texas, 25
Genoa, Italy, 39
Germany, 40, 58
gloves, *10*, 63
gold rush, 12, 41
Great Falls, Montana, 30
Gripper Snap, 34

hat:
    color of, 23
    decoration on, 14–15, *16*, 18
    felt, 11–13, *16*, 17–18, *19*, *20*, *21*
    mercury in, 12
    origin of, 11–12

    shape of, 11–12, *13*, 14–15, *16*,
        19, *20*, 23, *23*, *24*, 25, *ci5*
    straw, 11, 21–22, *22*
    uses of, 14–15
    see also Resistol hat, Stetson
        hat
hat production:
    bleaching, 22
    blending fur, 17–18
    blocking and pressing, 18, *20*,
        22
    dyeing, 18
    former, 17–18
    fur types, 11–12, 17–18
    hatter's oil, 18
    lining, 18, *20*, 22
    pouncing, 18
    powdering, 18
    shapes, 18, *19*, 22, *23*
    sharking, 18, *20*
    shellacking, 18, 22
    shrinking, 18
    singeing, 18
    sinker tub, 18
    sizing, 18, 21
    steaming, 18
    styling, 18
    sweatbands, 18, *20*, 22, 25
    trimming, 18, 22
H. J. Justin & Sons, Inc., 46, 56
Hollywood, 27

Italy, 58

Japan, 58
jeans:
    cut of, 44–45
    history of, 39–45
    rivets on, 42–43, 45
    popularity of, 39, 44–45
    sizing of, 42–45
    see also Lee, Levi's, Wrangler
jewelry, 68, *ci2*

John B. Stetson Company, 13, 25
Justin, Anis, 56
Justin, Annie, 55–56
Justin-Barton Belt Company, 68
Justin Belt Company, 68
Justin Boot Company, 54, *55*
Justin boots, *46, 47, 52,* 54–58,
    55, 57, 59, ci4
Justin, Earl, 56
Justin, Enid, 56–57
Justin, Fern, 56
Justin, H. J. "Joe", 50, 54–56
Justin, H. Joe, 54, 56–57
Justin Industries, Inc., 57, 68
Justin, John, 56
Justin, John, Jr., 57, 67–68
Justin, Myrl, 56
Justin, Sam, 56–57
Justin, Texas, 53

Kelly, Eddie, 58
Kiwanis, 32

Lafayette, Indiana, 54
Lee, 45
legends, 11–12, 39–41
Levi's:
    denim, 41–43
    501s 42–44, *44, ci7*
    557s 43–44
    history of, 40–44
    Lady Levi's, 43
    leather label on, 43, *45*
    overalls, 41–43, *42*
    red tab on, 43
    rivets on, 42–43
    sizing of, 42, 44
    stitching on, 43, *45*
Levi Strauss & Company, 7, 41,
    43, 44
Little Joe the Wrangler, 3, *3*
Lonesome Dove, 25

McCoy, Joe, 1
Miller and Company, 32
Miller, Phil, 31–32
Miller Stockman, 32
Mix, Tom, 25, 27, *ci5*
Montana, 62
Montana Silversmiths, 7

National Cowboy Hall of Fame
    and Western Heritage
    Center, 56
Navaho, 32
New England, 41
Nîme, France, 41
Nocona Boot Company, *49,* 56
Nocona, Texas, 55–56
Nogales, Arizona, 53
Nudie, 28

Oklahoma City, Oklahoma, 56

passing on the heritage, 4, *5,*
    24, 25, 35
Philadelphia, Pennsylvania,
    12–13
Phoenix, Arizona, 30
Pike's Peak, 12
Professional Rodeo Cowboy's
    Association, 45

rag, see bandanna
Red River, 3, 54
Reno, Nevada, 42

Resistol hat, *16, 19, 20, 21,* 25
Rockmount Ranch Wear Manu-
    facturing Company, *ii,* 7,
    26, 33, 34–36, *35, 36,* 68
rodeo:
    cowboys, 6, *29, 31, ci6, ci7, ci8*
    cowgirls, *15, 51, 65*
    life, *5,* 11, 28, 32, 45, 63, 65–66, 68

Rodriguez, Florentino, 53
Rogers, Roy, 28
Ropers, *viii, 26, 37, 51, 52, 59, 66,*
    69, ci4
Rotary Club, 32

Saint Joseph, Missouri, 12
Salt Lake City, Utah, 30
San Francisco, California, 34,
    41
scarfs, *see* bandannas
Scovill Manufacturing Com-
    pany, 34
serge de Nîme, 41
Sheplers, 7–8
shin plasters, 54
shirt pockets:
    smile, *26,* 34, *60*
    snap-button flap, *ii, viii, 6,*
        33, 34, *35*
shirts:
    bib front, 28, *29, 31*
    colors of, 27, 32
    cuffs on, *29, 33,* 34, *60*
    manufacturing of, 31–37
    materials for, 27, 32
    piping on, *26, 33, 33, 60*
    snap-button, *ii, viii, 6,* 7, *26,*
        29, 31, 33, 34, 37, *60*
    yoke on, *33,* 37, *60*
skirts, *ii, 15, 36, 65*
Socorro, New Mexico, 2

songs, 2–3, 50
Spanish Fort, Texas, 54
square dance costumes, *ii,* 36,
    36
Stern, David, 41
Stetson hat, *10,* 12–14, *16,* 25
Stetson, John B., 12–13
Strait, George, 25
Strauss, Levi, 39–43, *40*

Texas, 1–3, 32, 54, 61
Texas Rancher's Supply
    Company, 32
"These Boots Were Made for
    Walking," 50
Thorp, N. Howard, 2
Tibbs, Casey, 28, *29*
Tony Lama Boots, 49, 57

urban cowboy, 7, *16,* 68

vests, 7, *13, 28, 48, 63, 65*
V. F. Corporation, 45

Wayne, John, 28
Weil, Jack A., 30–35, *35*
Weil, Jack B., *35, 35*
Weil, Steven E., *26,* 35, *35*
wipes, *see* bandannas
World War II, 34, 43
Wrangler, 45
Wyoming, 62

ABOUT THE AUTHOR

M. Jean Greenlaw

is currently Regents Professor at the University of North Texas. She has coauthored several books on children's literature and education, contributed chapters to a number of other works, and published widely in professional periodicals. Among her many honors are the Arbuthnot Award for outstanding teaching of children's literature, given by the International Reading Association in 1992. *Ranch Dressing* is her first children's book. About it, she says: "Texas is my adopted state, and I became fascinated with the enduring nature of western wear. In my research, which covered three years and various states, I encountered many people who were generous with their time, knowledge, and stories. I have tried to capture the essence of their pride and their eagerness to tell the story of a clothing that survives as a symbol of the real West." Ms. Greenlaw lives in Denton, Texas, with her dog, Miff.